CHRISTMAS WONDER

Things to make, songs poems to say, food to bake, stories to learn and traditions to cherish.

Entertaining, educational and charming.

The all-about-Christmas book, brimming with craftwork, lore, poems, songs and stories. It will entertain and amuse both children and adults alike.

It evokes the traditional Christmas in city and countryside and takes the reader on a journey of wonder - from the lighting of the Christmas Eve Candle, to the colourful excitement of the Wren's Day, and includes stories about the Pantomime.

Maureen Potter, Polly Devlin, Eamonn MacThomáis, Paddy Crosbie, Frank O'Connor, Olive Sharkey and Edna Burrows entertain the reader with Christmas stories and traditions.

Drawings by Jole Bortoli (traditions) , Seán O'Leary (craft work), and Orlagh Murphy (Christmas in other lands) decorate the book.

Seán C. O'Leary

CHRISTMAS WONDER

From Ireland — for Children

Craftwork, Lore, Poems, Songs and Stories

Illustrations
Jole Bortoli, Seán C. O'Leary,
Orlagh Murphy

THE O'BRIEN PRESS
DUBLIN

First published 1988 by The O'Brien Press Ltd.,
20 Victoria Road, Dublin 6, Ireland
©

British Library Cataloguing in Publication Data
O'Leary, Sean C.
Christmas Wonder: from Ireland—for children:
Craftwork, lore, poems, songs and stories.
1. Christmas activities—Collections
—For children 790.1
ISBN 0-86278-177-9

Design and layout : The Graphiconies
Printing : SciPrint Ltd., Shannon

10 9 8 7 6 5 4 3 2 1

For my daughter Suzy
who thankfully still knows
the wonder of Christmas

Contents

Illustrations

Jole Bortoli created and drew the illustrations on the
following pages : 1, 3, 4, 5, 7, 8, 9, 10, 12, 14, 15, 16,
17, 21 (after Brian Bourke), 26, 30, 34, 38, 39, 40, 41,
43, 48, 56, 61 (top), 62 (bottom), 65, 67, 77, 87, 96
(after David Rooney).

Sean C. O'Leary planned, conceived and drew the
craft illustrations on the following pages : 13, 18, 19,
20, 31, 32, 37, 45, 50, 51, 52, 53, 54, 55, 57, 58, 59,
60, 61 (bottom), 62 (top) , 63.

Orlagh Murphy drew the illustrations on
pages : 71, 75, 81, 85.

Introduction

Our Granny comes to stay with us every Christmas. She's our Dad's Mum. She travels up from the country by train. When the train arrives, she stays in her seat beside a window and we run excitedly along the platform from carriage to carriage until we find her. She always has a big suitcase and lots of parcels.

As we travel home through the city, she is always amazed at the bright Christmas lights and the noise and crush in the streets. 'Such a difference, children, to when I, or even your father, was a child,' she murmurs in a faraway voice, half to us and half to herself.

In the days before Christmas, while Mum and Dad are out at work, Granny takes charge of decorating the tree, getting the crib and candle ready and icing the cake. As we all work together she tells us stories about Christmas long ago and shows us how to make wonderful Christmas things. We have a great time. We keep on asking her for more until in the end she gets tired and says,

'Ah children! Give me a rest. Put the kettle on and when I've had a cup of tea and a few of those chocolate biscuits, we might have some more of the wonder.'

This is our Granny's book of CHRISTMAS WONDER.

The Christmas Candle

Well, children, on Christmas Eve we remember that Mary and Joseph were on the last part of their journey to Bethlehem. When they arrived they could not find anywhere to stay. Nobody would give them shelter. They felt very worried and lonely and had to spend the night in a stable, where Jesus was born.

In every house in Ireland long ago a lighted candle was placed in the window, on Christmas Eve, in memory of that journey. The candlelight would glow softly and shyly in the winter dark as a sign of welcome to Mary and Joseph.

Your great-grandad, or Pa as we used to call him, would take us up to the top of the hill opposite the house to gaze down in wonder at the valley flickering with light. Every household had a candle lighting, and in lots of the houses there was a candle in every window. Tears would flow down Pa's cheeks as the beauty of the scene touched him and he remembered his own brothers and sisters and their past happy Christmases.

One of Mother's first jobs on Christmas Eve was to get the Christmas candle or as we called it, *Coinneal Mór na Nollag*, ready. We all gathered around the kitchen table to watch her and knew that Christmas was really starting.

She would take the biggest turnip she could find, and after washing and drying it, scrape out a hole in the centre. Into this would go the big red Christmas candle. Then she would tie some tinsel at the top and wind it down around the body of the candle, tying it again at the end. She would poke a few holes in different places around the turnip and stick in bits of holly. When that was done, it was placed on the wide window-sill in the kitchen and finished off by putting more holly around the edge and sticking paper flowers in it. We thought it was wonderful.

That evening, about six o'clock, when most of the work was done, all the family would gather together to light the candle.

First we would kneel and say a prayer for those living and dead. Then the youngest, that was my sister Bridie, would light the candle and as she did, Pa would say *'Go mbeirimíd beo ag an am seo arís'* - May we all live to see this day next year.

Then we children would scramble to our places at the table and tuck into a tea of barmbrack, seed loaf and cake. Christmas had started.

The Story of Tinsel

Mary and Joseph's journey to Bethlehem was long and dangerous. They were always afraid of being attacked by robbers and thieves.

One evening, tired and hungry, they took shelter in a cave. A little spider lived in the cave and when he saw how miserable and frightened they were, he decided to help them in the only way he knew. He would stay guard all night. So scuttling to the mouth of the cave, he spun his web right across the entrance and then settled down to watch.

The night was bitterly cold and soon the web became covered in frost.

Later on that night a band of thieves came by looking for a cave to sleep in. They noticed the frosted web glittering in the moonlight but passed on thinking that such a cave must be very damp and dusty. Mary and Joseph were saved.

And so we remember the little spider's good deed when we wind the silver tinsel around the Christmas candle.

Christmas Flowers

You Will Need

1 Tissue paper in different colours
2 Some narrow drinking straws
3 Sellotape

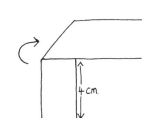

What To Do

A For each flower you will need to cut a piece of tissue paper 8cm wide and at least 45cm long. The longer the piece of tissue, the bigger the flower.

B Fold the paper in half, lengthways.

C Leaving about 4cm at the end, fold over and crease the tissue to make a right-angle, as shown. Fold and crease it forward again to make another right-angle. Then forward and over once more. You will then have formed a square. Fold the tissue in such a way as to leave a tiny hole in the centre.

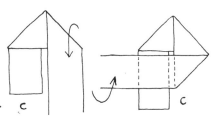

D Keep on folding and creasing the tissue in this way, forming square on top of square until you reach the end. Cut off any leftover bit. While folding be careful not to cover over the centre hole.

E Turn the stack of squares over and push the straw up through the centre hole. Sellotape the end of it to the piece of tissue you left over at the beginning.

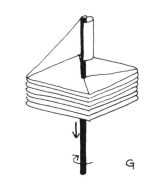

F Holding the straw in your right hand, put your left thumb and first finger underneath the squares of tissue.

G Gently pull the straw through the centre hole and at the same time twist it round and round to form the flower. Then stick a piece of sellotape around the straw and tissue just underneath the flower to stop it unwinding.

H Cut straw to required length.

Long, Long Ago

Winds through the olive trees
Softly did blow,
Round little Bethlehem,
Long, long ago.

Sheep on the hillside lay
Whiter than snow,
Shepherds were watching them,
Long, long ago.

Then from the happy skies,
Angels bent low,
Singing their songs of joy,
Long, long ago.

For in a manger bed,
Cradled we know,
Christ came to Bethlehem,
Long, long ago

Katherine Parker

Christmas Candle Table-centre

You Will Need

1 An empty jam-jar and enough earth or sand to fill it

2 Medium-sized candle suitable for use at table. If the candle is too big or tall it will topple over the jar   3 Coloured sugar paper

What To Do

A Place candle in jar and keep in place by packing the earth or sand around it. Be sure that it is steady.

B Cut a piece of sugar paper a few cm wider than the height of the jar and long enough to fit loosely around the jar, allowing for an overlap.

C Pleat the paper into approx. 3cm-wide pleats.

D Keep pleats together and shape top using scissors. Different shapes can be cut - star, flame, point etc.

E Open out pleats. Brush some paste on the shaped tops & sprinkle on glitter.

F Put pleated paper loosely around jam-jar, overlap edges and paste together.

G Group a number of candles together, of different heights and colours, using matching or contrasting paper to form a very pretty table-centre.

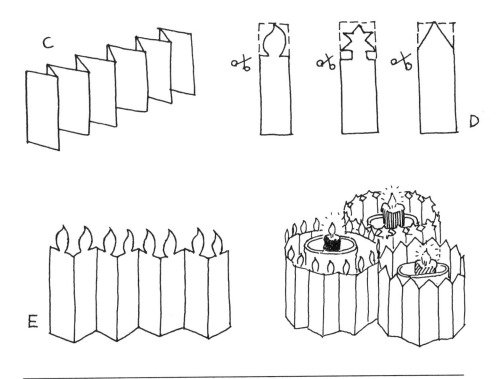

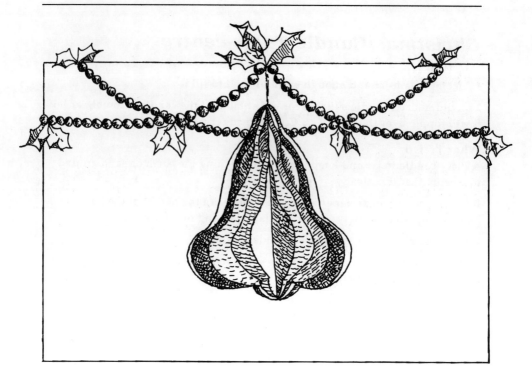

Decorations

A couple of days before Christmas Eve, Pa and John-Joe, my elder brother, would bring back bundles of holly from Crinken Wood and dump them on the floor in the kitchen. We younger children - there were thirteen of us in all - could hardly contain ourselves with excitement. We'd get any old tin or bowl or saucer we could find and start making little collections of the red holly berries. Mother would organise us with needles and thread and for the rest of the night we'd be threading the leaves and berries into strands. All the while we would tell stories and jokes and sing scraps of songs we had learned from Pa. Every now and then the fun would be interrupted by the squeal of someone who had pricked their finger with the needle and the rest of us would chant, 'You'll be better before you're twice married!'

After every two or three strands were finished, mother would tie them together to make one long strand. She'd hang these longer strands across the top of the dresser, over the windows, above the fire, anywhere that took her fancy. In between each loop she'd put a little bunch of holly with paper flowers stuck in it. Mother and my older sister, Mary-Ann, always made these little flowers because they were the handiest with their fingers.

By bedtime we'd have the whole house decorated, ready for Christmas Day. Mother would heat us up some milk and while we were drinking it Pa would tell us one of his ghost stories. Afterwards we'd scamper to bed, tricking and fooling and scaring each other as we went. We were a happy bunch. Some of that thirteen are dead now, and a good deal of the others scattered all over the world in England, America, Australia and other places.

Much later on when I was married myself and your father was a boy, we got the first paper decorations in Woolworth's shop. We stopped threading the leaves and berries then. There was one decoration in particular that your father loved and that was a paper bell I always hung in the hall. He'd gaze at it in wonder and one Christmas when I was taking down the decorations I let him have it for himself. I wouldn't be surprised if he still has it!

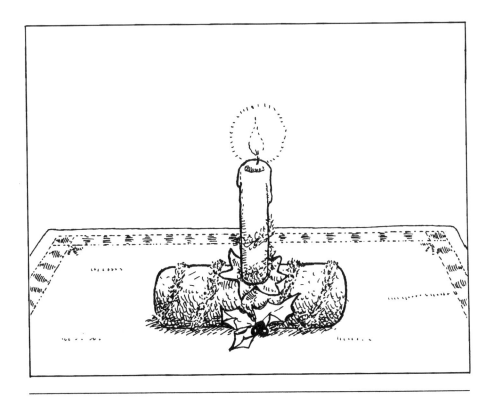

Holly Garlands

YOU WILL NEED

1 Holly with plenty of red berries

2 Needle and thread

WHAT TO DO

A Pick a little pile of red berries and a little pile of green leaves from the holly.

B Thread the needle with the required length of thread. Tie a double knot about 6cm from the end. Use a thin needle. A thick one will burst the berries.

C Thread the berries and leaves as shown. Leave about six to eight berries between each leaf. Finish off about 6cm from the needle and tie a double knot. Hang.

D Try different combinations of leaves and berries.

Christmas Bell

YOU WILL NEED

1 Five half-sheets of tissue paper in different colours (a half-sheet of tissue paper is about 50cm x 38cm)

2 Paste. Pritt Stick paste is ideal for this activity

3 Piece of light cardboard. Thread for hanging

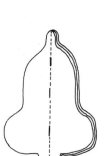

D

WHAT TO DO

A Cut the bell shape out of the cardboard using the template on page 19.

B Fold each half-sheet of tissue-paper in four and stack the folded sheets on top of one another.

C Put the cardboard bell on top and trace all around with a pencil. Cut around this outline, through the tissue, to make 20 bell shapes.

D Keeping the bell shapes stacked together, fold them along the centre line. Crease. Open out and staple right through in three places along the crease. Lay flat on table.

E Except for the very top piece, trim about 1cm off

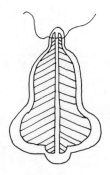

F

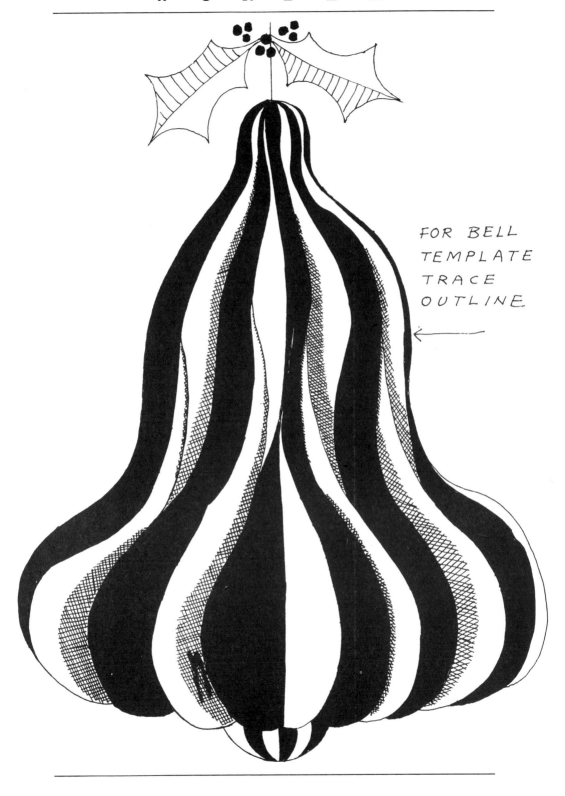

FOR BELL
TEMPLATE
TRACE
OUTLINE

the cardboard bell shape all around. Cut it in two along the centre line. Make a little hole at the top of each half and put a fairly long piece of thread through the two holes, leaving it to lie loosely.

F With thread in place, paste each half to the pile of tissue bell shapes. Do not paste at the top where the thread is.

G Turn bell shapes over. Put a dab of paste at the top of the left side of the first bell shape. Fold the right side over on to this and smooth into place.

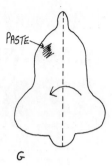

G

This right side has now become a left side. Put a dab of paste at the bottom of this new left side and fold the next right side over onto it.

Continue in this way, every second turn putting paste at the top and bottom of the left sides and folding the right sides over onto them.

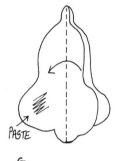

G

Work the whole way to the right. Return to the centre. Now work the whole way to the left, this time putting the paste on the right sides and folding the left sides over on to them.

H When finished, paste the two pieces of cardboard together. This will open out the bell. Tie a loop in the thread and hang bell. Open out each section so that the bell is even all around.

If preferred, the bell can be hung flat against the wall without pasting the two pieces of cardboard together.

The Holly and Ivy Girl

Come, buy my nice fresh ivy, and my holly boughs so green,
I have the fairest branches that ever yet were seen.
Come, buy from me, good Christians, and let me home, I pray,
And I'll wish you a merry Christmas time and a happy New Year's Day.

Ah! Won't you take my ivy? the loveliest ever seen.
Ah! Won't you have my holly boughs? all you that love the green.
Do! Take a little bunch of each, and on my knees I'll pray,
That God may bless your Christmas, and be with you New Year's Day.

Kerry in the 1900's

Christmas in the area near Dingle in the early 1900s was a much simpler affair than it is today. Here Jimeen, that madcap mischief-maker, describes the days before Christmas around 1919, and tells how he and his sister Cait decorated their home.

Jimeen Prepares for Christmas

I must tell you about the Christmas we had. Mam went to Dingle a few days before it - herself and Dad - and they took the horse and cart, with a creel and a box in the cart.

Mam had the money, and she took two geese - one for the vet and one for the bank manager, because he's the man who minds her money and she thinks the world of him.

While they were in Dingle, I went off to Glenadown with the big knife and some string and brought home a big holly bush, and I got some ivy in the ruins of the church.

As I was passing her door, Nell-Mary-Andy came out and was buttering me up trying to get me to give her some holly. She thought she'd make a right little eejit of me, praising me and calling me a 'good little boy', and promising me a Christmas present! I pretended, at first, that I wouldn't give her any. But, when I untied the bundle at home, I took a couple of branches over. I'm very great with Nell, you know.

Cait was all excited when she saw the big load I was bringing in.

'Oh!,' said she, 'we'll make the house lovely,' and she was looking at the red berries on the holly and dancing around the floor.

'Oh, aren't they beautiful?' said she. 'Did you ever see such a lovely red?'

That's the way Cait always goes on, even if it's only a daisy or a bunch of cowslips. All the girls are like that, about all kinds of things.

I was hungry.

'Stop your messing,' said I, 'is there anything to eat?'

'Oh! I forgot,' said Cait and she began to whisper. 'You won't tell what I've made, will you?'

'What?' said I.

She laughed.

'I won't tell you, because you'd tell Mam.'

'I swear I won't,' said I.

'She'll kill me over the sugar,' said Cait.

'What sugar?' said I.

'And because of the cream!' said she.

'Crikey, Cait, have you made sweet cakes!'

'I won't tell you, I won't tell you,' said she, laughing and jumping up and down. Then she went to the dresser and took down two cups.

'Ah! Cait,' said I, 'tell me what you made.'

'I won't, I won't,' said she, and she laughed, dancing and kicking up her heels. She didn't see the ivy on the floor until it tripped her up and, lo and behold, didn't she break a big piece off the rim of one of the cups.

Cait picked it up and she was trembling as she tried to fix it back in place. She started to cry, and then didn't she try to put the blame on me! I soon told her that it was herself and her jumping around. But there was no point in talking. All she'd do was cry.

I ended up feeling sorry for her.

'Give it to me, Cait,' said I, 'and Mam won't ever know about it.'

I took the cup to the dresser and put it under two other cups with the broken side facing in.

'What will I do if Mam finds it?' said Cait.

Then we each had a mug of tea. That was when Cait brought out the things she'd made - little cream cakes with sugar icing on them. We got butter in the cupboard and I spotted a big pot of jam with the top tied tight. I cut the knot easily and we enjoyed all the things we had. We put a full spoon of jam on every bit of bread.

When we'd eaten our fill, the jam was well down the pot, but I tied the paper on again and put it back in the cupboard where it had been. It's a pity Mam doesn't go to Dingle every day!

Then I got a hammer and little nails and Cait handed me the holly and ivy. We nailed it around the window, on top of the dresser, and over the fireplace. It was hard to fix it where there was no wood, and I had to drive big nails into the wall. From time to time huge chunks of mortar fell.

When we'd finished the house, we grabbed Sailor - that's the dog - and covered him head to tail with holly, and had a great laugh at him. When evening came we lit the lamp. The house looked lovely.

It was dark when Mam and Dad came home. We thought Mam'd be delighted but, to tell the truth, she caused ructions when she saw the lumps of mortar missing from the walls. I had to disappear until she calmed down. It's hard to please some people!

From Jimeen, Pádraig O Siochfhradha (An Seabhac)

Christmas in Dublin

Paddy Crosbie grew up in the early 1900s in the centre of Dublin city. In those days Dublin was very poor, and finding money for presents must have been very difficult. Still, everyone enjoyed Christmas.

Dublin in the 1920s

Christmas in Dublin was Christmas no matter what trouble or war was on. During the very poor period up to about 1920, toys were very scarce in all homes. Rag dolls, many of them home-made, and wooden toys like engines, were the usual ones for girls and boys respectively. Stockings were hung up, however, on Christmas Eve, no matter how bleak the outlook.

I got a meccano set, No. 1A, in 1920 that I cherished and kept intact for years. Mona got her first real doll the same year, one with a smooth rosy face and a head of hair. The body was just rag and sawdust. When Mossy and I were altarboys, Christmas morning was a very busy one as each priest 'said' three Masses. But there was electricity in the air.

The days before Christmas were full of magic. Woolworth's, 'the 3d and 6d store', was a fairyland to all children and unknown to our parents some of the gang and myself often sneaked down town to wander up and down through the counters in Woolworth's store. We eyed the toys enviously . . . and dreamed of stockings full to the top with the toys on show. We paid visits also to a small bazaar on the other side of Henry Street. There were no fairy lights strung across the street, but the well-lit windows of every shop in Henry Street and Mary Street satisfied us to the full.

From Your Dinner's Poured Out, Paddy Crosbie

Twenty years later things were a bit easier. Eamonn MacThomáis, growing up in Dublin in the 1940s, tells how the children eyed the toys in the shops before Christmas.

Dublin in the 1940s

A Chiseller's Christmas

We may not have been able to count the weeks or months to Easter or Whit, or even to St Patrick's Day, but we always knew when it was only twelve weeks to Christmas. Clarke's sweet and toy shop at the top of Bulfin Road had both windows full of a vast selection of toys. Each item had its own label, telling its own story.

A red fire engine with a yellow ladder three shillings . . . A swarm of children, with our noses stuck to the glass window and our warm breaths in the cold October air fogging up the window panes. Then polishing the window with the sleeves of our coats and listening to the chorus of voices all shouting:

'I'm getting that, and that, and maybe I'll get that, but I'm defney getting that.'. . .

We seldom missed a Sunday's visit as the shop was only a few paces from St Michael's Church, and even on a weekday a special visit would be made just to see again the toys we dreamed would be in our stockings at the foot of the bed on Christmas morning.

On Christmas Eve, the girl next door would come in to help me write my letter to Santa Claus. She would dictate the letter and address the envelope, but when she insisted that I put down a blue sports racing car with the number of my hall door (30) on it, I threw down the pencil.

'I want a red fire engine with a yellow ladder,' I said. 'I don't want a blue racing car, even if it has our hall door number on it.'

God bless Bernie, she's a Poor Clare nun today in Belfast, but she had great patience in those days. The battle between the blue racing car and the red fire engine was not won that Christmas Eve as I ran upstairs saying I was going to wait up all night and if Mister Santa Claus tried to off-load his old blue racing car into my stocking I'd give him a good kick.

I remember fighting the sandman that night. The sandman was the man (invisible) who went around at night time throwing sand into your eyes to make you sleep or blind you. But the sandman had won the battle and when I awoke the following morning there was the bloody blue racing car sticking out of my stocking at the end of the bed. I cursed Santa a few times and then noticed a little mouth organ and the sweets in the other stocking. I was told later that this was Santa's way of saying 'sorry', that he must have had only one red fire engine and that he had given it to a poor little boy with no mammy and daddy. . . .

After Mass that Christmas morning I rushed over to Clarke's toy shop. Both windows were empty. The red fire engine with the yellow ladders was gone. Old Mrs Clarke, Lord rest her, told me that Santa had collected all the toys last night and she didn't know where the poor little boy lived who had got the fire engine.

I think that was the only Christmas I was disappointed. The following year I got the red fire engine with the yellow ladder and I wondered if the poor little boy got the blue racing car. I didn't seem to mind what other children got and I never cursed Santa for giving bigger presents to other children. The way I looked at it was that if you got what you asked for you were happy.

From Gur Cake and Coal Blocks, Eamonn MacThomáis

Here Eamonn MacThomáis tells us about the preparations for Christmas - the food, the decorations, the visit to Santa.

The Days before Christmas

The twelve weeks to Christmas were spent in joyful mood, singing songs or visiting shop windows or the trip to town to see Santa Claus and climb the stone steps of Nelson's Pillar . . .

We were well on the streets with the spirit of Christmas long before the real carol singers and musicians appeared. The shop windows with their white cotton wool made to look like snow; the rows of candied peel, currants, raisins, cherries and all the lovely things for making the plum pudding. The butcher shops with their turkeys and geese hanging from silver hooks. The cake shop with its massive range of Christmas cakes: Oxford Lunches wrapped in silver paper, and the large biscuit tin holder decorated with holly and ivy. Each biscuit tin had a glass lid so that you could see at a glance the variety of cream custard and jam biscuits. Even the hardware stores were decorated with coloured paper chains and the long red Christmas candles were given pride of place in the window. Very few houses had fairy lights or Christmas trees in those days, so we feasted our eyes on the chemist shop window which was aglow in coloured lights, giving new magic to their displays of toilet soaps, manicure sets, combs and brushes. An odd big house on the South Circular Road had a Christmas tree and I stood for hours at the gate, looking at the tree in the window with its coloured lights going on and off every few seconds. The finest sight to my childish eyes was Santa Claus, his reindeer and sleigh of toys in coloured lights high up on the wall above McBirney's shop on Aston Quay . . .

The visit to Santa was made wherever Santa had the cheapest parcels. Prices ranged from sixpence to two shillings. Whatever shop Santa was in, he had his own Toyland, and I've yet to see today anything that could come up to the standard of those childhood years.

From Gur Cake and Coal Blocks, Eamonn MacThomáis

Christmas Cards and Parcels

Long ago, it was the cards that warmed the heart at Christmas with news from family and friends, especially from those in America and Australia. All work would stop when the post came. Often there'd be a letter in with the card, and maybe even a few dollars. Mother would sit by the fire and read out the letters to the whole family and we'd talk and discuss them for ages. She'd read them out again that night and the following day and several times over Christmas, and pass them on to any of the neighbours who had been especially friendly with the writer.

In those days, when people went to work in America and Australia they hardly ever came home again. They had barely enough money to get there not to talk about coming home. We really looked forward to their cards and letters, especially at Christmas. Of course we sent them the same and we always had to be sure to post them well in advance. You'd nearly post a card for Australia in September!

If any of them did well out there, they might send you a parcel. Your Grandad, Lord have mercy on his soul, had a brother who went out to California. Every year, after he had got married himself, he used to send us a big flat box of dried American fruit. Rows and rows of yellow pineapples and orange apricots and fruits whose names we never found out. It was like a box of sunshine. The first time it came we didn't know what to make of it. We had never seen anything like it before. We were afraid to eat them but Hannah McCarthy, a cousin of mine who had spent some time in the States, soon put us right. It was nice to think that he had done well enough to be able to send it to us. Of course Christmas wasn't Christmas after that until the Californian box arrived. And it always came. He's dead now, of course.

The cards and letters don't mean as much nowadays. With telephones and aeroplanes people are much more in contact with one another throughout the year. They come and go from America and Australia all the time now. I might even take a trip myself this coming spring. But when your father was growing up, and especially when I was a child myself, they meant a lot.

A Young Tradition

The tradition of sending cards at Christmastime is only about 150 years old. The first Christmas card is said to have been designed in London by Sir Henry Cole in 1846. It showed a happy family scene and the message read 'A Merry Christmas and a Happy New Year to You'. Not long afterwards, with the introduction of a postal service and the invention of cheaper ways of colour-printing, sending Christmas cards became very popular. It is still very popular today.

Christmas Cards

YOU WILL NEED

1 White cartridge paper is best but any paper will do as long as it is not too light

2 Coloured pencils or markers

3 Paste. Pritt Stick paste is ideal

4 Small bit of silver paper. Glitter and some made-up wallpaper paste

WHAT TO DO
Card 1

A Fold an 15 x 11 inch (38x28cm approx) sheet of cartridge paper in four to make a card.

B Cut out a piece of cartridge paper the same size as the front of the card.

C Fold and crease it in two lengthways. Open out and draw tree shape. Cut out and decorate.

D Stick tree to card as shown. Close card and smooth down. Write in greeting and any other decoration. When open, lay card flat on table.

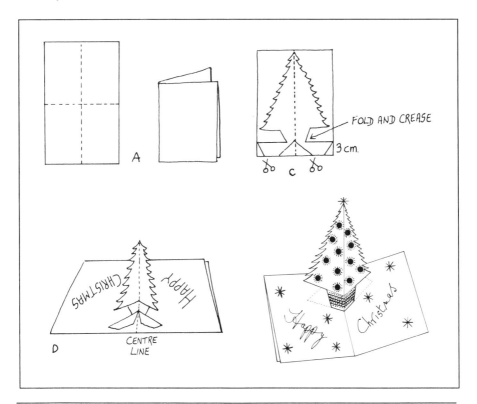

Card 2

A Fold and crease a 15 x 11inch (38X28cm) sheet of cartridge paper as shown.

B Find the centre point by measuring and fold each side inwards to it. Crease.

C Open card out completely and fold side-pieces around the back.

D Draw in candle shapes and cut as shown. Crease each candle shape over and back several times along its length.

E Open card out completely. Fold top half behind lower half. Crease.

F Fold the side pieces towards the centre, making sure the candle shapes pop out.

G Cut flame shapes from the silver paper. Fold in two lengthways and crease. Paste to the inside of the top of the candles.

H Decorate each candle using glitter and coloured pencils/markers. Write in greeting. When dry, close card and smooth all over.

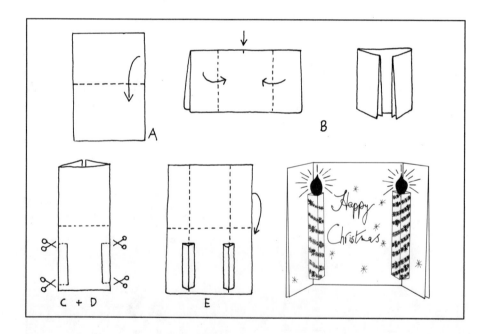

We all know how exciting it is to get a parcel, especially if it comes from abroad. Here, Polly Devlin tells us about Mary-Ellen, whose family have received a surprise parcel from America. They are all very excited. The father has just cut the string and begun to open the parcel.

The Opening of the Parcel

Their mother saved the stamps, and the string, and the first wrapping of paper inside the box which was an American newspaper. Inside of that was another big box and when that was opened there was white tissue-paper around a man's suit of clothes.

Underneath that, in bundles and packages, was a set of clothes for every child, with labels and names. Mary-Ellen's mother kept saying, as they were lifted out one by one - a red pleated skirt like a kilt for Kathleen, a blue dress with a white collar for Bridget, a blue skirt with pleats and braces for Teresa, and white rabbits embroidered on the waistband, check waistcoats and trousers for the boys - half laughing and half crying, 'How is it that our Ellie knows all our ones' names and ages so well? What's come over her sending us all this, and never a word from her these years?'

There was a white woolly coat for Mary-Ellen, that felt somewhat like fur, and each girl had a pair of white ankle-socks with a pattern round the tops. That was the first time Mary-Ellen had ever seen ankle-socks, for all the girls wore black knitted stockings at that time. There was a knitted jacket and blouse and skirt for their mother. Then, when everyone had got their parcels, there at the very bottom of the box was another box with Mary-Ellen's name on it. Her mother lifted it out and gave it to Mary-Ellen without opening it. Mary-Ellen was afraid to open it. Her brothers and sisters were all watching her in a ring, and her mother and father standing behind them, but they said go on, and she went down on her hunkers and opened the box. There was tissue-paper and a card on the top and on it was written:'To one Mary-Ellen from another' and her mother read it out and said, 'Our May-Ellie's name was by rights Mary-Ellen, the same as you.

I called you after her.'

Then Mary-Ellen opened the tissue-paper which had light gold stars printed on it. And inside the paper a doll was lying, with golden curly hair and closed eyes with black lashes and a white dress, white socks, black shoes and a necklace round her neck. Mary-Ellen looked at the doll, and sighed.

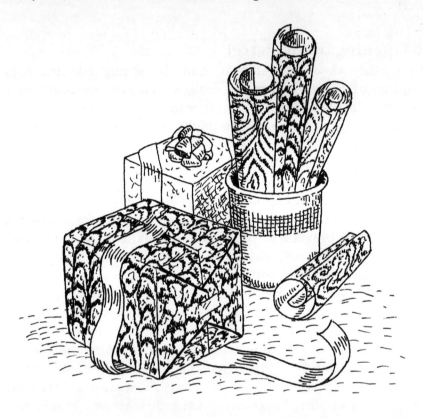

Her mother said, 'Lift it out,' and Mary-Ellen put her hands into the paper and lifted the doll out, and as she did so, the doll's eyes opened wide, as blue as blue. She would never forget it looking back at her. She nearly dropped the doll but still no one spoke. Then Mary-Ellen said, 'Is it mine?'

'It is yours,' her mother said.

'And can I keep it?' Mary-Ellen said.

And when her mother said, 'You can so, it's yours,' and Philomena the sister just older than Mary-Ellen began to cry for wanting it, Mary-Ellen knew it was hers, and everyone began talking.

The girls all wanted to look at the doll, but at the same time they wanted to try on their new clothes. Their mother went into the room to put on the new jacket and skirt and the white blouse with its high neck, and when she came out everyone stared at her and their father put his hand on her shoulder in a way Mary-Ellen had never seen before. And then all the sisters and brothers except Mary-Ellen ran in to put on their new clothes, and at the very end, their father went into the room, and put on the new suit, and when he came out, they all clapped him and themselves and their mother.

Mary-Ellen was still kneeling, holding her doll and watching, and laughing, and her mother bent down and told her to let Philomena hold the doll till she changed into her new coat. She didn't want to, in case she never got the doll back.

'Any other time,' Mary-Ellen said, 'I would have been over the moon about the white coat - but I could only think of the doll and I was out of that room and changed like the Creggan White Hare, to get the doll back from Philomena.'

Then their mother said, 'There's going to be no tea the night with all this consate [conceit] and admiring, away into the room and out of your new clothes, the fire will be dead on us.'

And so slowly they all changed back into their old clothes and sat down to eat, although Mary-Ellen could hardly eat.

From 'The China Doll', Polly Devlin

Christmas on a farm in the Midlands of Ireland sixty years ago is described by Olive Sharkey. Nowadays an orange would not be an exciting gift, but in those days foreign fruit was very rare.

Christmas in the Midlands

Festive fare was a very important consideration when planning for the various festivals during the year. One of the biggest celebrations took place at Christmas, and for that no expense was spared. My father relates how Christmas was celebrated in his home when he was young [in the 1920s]. Preparations began well in advance of Christmas week itself. Food was bought in bulk, the house was given a thorough 'going-over' with dusters and brushes, and large-scale baking was done almost every day. However, nothing festive was consumed until Christmas Eve, when a specially baked fruit cake was eaten by the family shortly after the *coinneal mór* (big candle, usually red) was lit and placed in the kitchen window.

Santy came during the night of course; in those days the toys in the sack were often homemade, and the traditional Christmas stocking was invariably filled with sticks of candy called 'Peggy's legs' and with lucky bags. Fruit, too, figured strongly, usually an orange or some other exotic fruit which might not be seen by the youngsters until the following Christmas. Early on Christmas morning the frying pan would be heard sizzling over the flames in the hearth as the traditional Christmas morning steak was cooked for the man of the house. After early Mass the housewife got to work on the preparation of the dinner. The goose or bronze turkey was cooked in the bastable (pot-oven) pot, bubbling away under a lid of constantly renewed hot coals throughout the morning. Outside in a nearby field the men and *garsúns* worked up an appetite with a game of 'shinny' (a rudimentary game of hurling) and went to their respective homes in the early afternoon feeling ravenous.

The man of the house was presented with the first huge mug of green goose soup, then the remainder of the gathering received theirs in tin panniers. The first course dispensed with, the family tucked into the main dinner, which consisted of generous slices of goose, potatoes, vegetables, and sometimes a thick, greasy gravy. Porter was served to all age groups to wash the food down, a special concession to the children in some homes on this important feastday. Afterwards, porter cake was served with tea to anyone who could manage it.

From Old Days, Old Ways, Olive Sharkey

Paper for Wrapping Gifts

YOU WILL NEED

1 Two tubes of artists' oil paint in two contrasting colours

2 White spirit

3 About a dessertspoonful of dry wallpaper paste

4 Plastic basin - square if possible and as large as you can find

5 Two paste brushes or thick paint brushes - one for each colour

6 White cartridge paper. If necessary cut it so that it will fit in the basin

7 Two empty yoghurt cartons or old cups. Teaspoon.

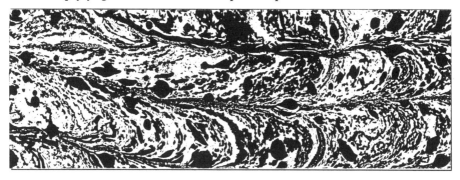

WHAT TO DO

A Fill the basin with cold water to within 2 inches (5cm) of the top. Sprinkle on the wallpaper paste and briskly mix it in. Leave for about 10 minutes and stir briskly again. The wallpaper paste will slightly thicken the water.

B Squeeze a little of the paint into the yoghurt cartons. One colour to each carton. Add some white spirit and stir well with the brush until all the colour is mixed in. Do not make the mixture too watery or your design will be very pale in colour.

C Using a separate brush for each colour and taking up plenty of paint on the brush, dribble and shake spots of each colour all over the water. Then with the teaspoon mingle the colours together and gently trace out a design on the surface of the water.

D Lay the paper carefully on top of the paint. Leave for a second. Then holding it by two corners slowly lift it up. Your paper will have a colourful design printed on it. When dry use it to wrap your presents. Use a matching ribbon or piece of wool for tying your parcel.

E With practice you can use more than two colours and make really exciting designs.

Helping with the Christmas Baking

Cake Frill

YOU WILL NEED

1 Coloured paper in two contrasting colours - green/red, blue/white, green/white etc.

2 Paste. Pritt Stick paste is ideal

WHAT TO DO

A Cut two strips of paper in two different colours. The width of the strips must be the same as the height of the cake, and their length long enough to go around the cake, allowing for a small (3cm) overlap.

B Fold one of the strips into 7cm or 8cm-wide pleats.

C Keeping the pleats together cut out snowman or tree shape. Other shapes can be tried. Do not cut where shown.

D Open out pleats and paste to other strip of paper.

E Put frill around cake and keep in place with a dab of paste or a pin.

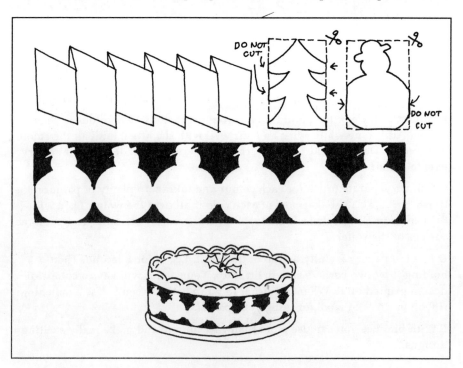

Mince Pie Stars

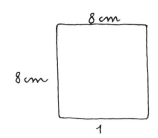

1

YOU WILL NEED

6 oz plain flour

4 oz margarine or butter

1/4 teaspoon salt

2 tablespoons of cold water

Some mincemeat. A jar of mincemeat can be bought at a supermarket

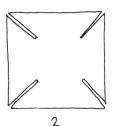

2

WHAT TO DO

A Wash your hands thoroughly.

B Put the oven on at 230°C/450°F, gas mark 7.

C Sift flour and salt together into a mixing bowl.

D Cut margarine or butter into little pieces and put them in with the flour.

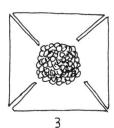

3

E With fingers, mix the flour and margarine together until it becomes like breadcrumbs.

F Add the water and mix to stiff dough. Roll and pat the dough into a firm ball.

G Sprinkle flour on the worktop and rub some on your rolling pin. Put ball in the centre of flour and roll the dough out fairly thinly.

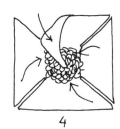

4

H Cut into squares (approx. 8cm) with a knife.

I Cut corners of squares as shown. Put 1/2 teaspoon of mincemeat in the centre and fold into star shape. After each point is folded over, dab it with water so that the next point sticks to it.

J Put stars on baking tray and bake for 15 minutes. Be careful not to leave them in any longer or the points will burn.

Tasty and mouth-watering!

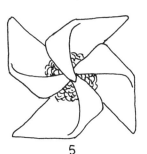

5

After-Christmas-dinner Mints

YOU WILL NEED

8 oz icing sugar (approx. 2 cups)

White of one egg in a cup

Peppermint essence

Sieve, mixing bowl, wooden spoon, fork, rolling pin, large plate, small cutters

WHAT TO DO

A Wash your hands thoroughly.

B Sieve the icing sugar into the bowl.

C Whisk the white of egg for a little while with a fork.

D Bit by bit, add the white of egg to the sugar, mixing well until you have a stiff but not wet paste. You may not need all the egg white.

E Mix in two or three drops of peppermint essence.

F Sprinkle some icing sugar on the worktop. Put the paste on it and knead well with the heel of your hand. Then roll it into a ball.

G Sprinkle some more sugar on the worktop and on the rolling pin. Roll out the paste, using the rolling pin, until it is 1/4 inch (6mm) in thickness.

H Cut into shapes using the cutters. Put on the plate, cover and leave to dry overnight.

Delicious!

For an extra treat, melt a bar of plain chocolate in a small saucepan over *very* low heat. Do not allow it to boil or burn. Dip half of each peppermint in the chocolate. Allow chocolate to harden.

The Crib

When I was a child growing up we never had a crib, but when your father was a boy they were very common. In fact he was the one in the house who put up the crib.

The first crib we had was made of cardboard. My sister Angela, who was a nun in America, sent it to us. It was lovely. When you opened it up all the figures stood up and you'd think it was a real place. We used to put it on the shelf beside the wireless - that was what we called a radio in those days. I have this memory of your father listening to the wireless on Christmas Eve, hoping that his name would be called out on Santa's list, and all the while gazing in wonder at the cardboard crib. In the centre was the Baby, with Mary and Joseph, and all around were hills and forests with little pathways through them. Along these pathways came people of all sorts, shepherds, kings, tradesmen, animals, coming to visit Jesus and bringing him gifts. Overhead, crowds of angels sang and blew trumpets while two of them carried a scroll, stretched right across the top of the crib, which said, *'Gloria in Excelsis Deo'* - Praise be to God.

Later on we bought little figures in Woolworth's shop and every year your Dad would make a different stable or cave to put them in. He'd numb his fingers picking moss on the damp banks and ditches to make a bed for the Baby Jesus, and drag ivy from the orchard wall to decorate the outside of the cave. When the electricity was put in the houses, we bought fairy lights and put them inside and outside the crib, making it into a wonderland.

Every Christmas, your Dad and his friends would go around from house to house viewing all the different cribs. Some people went to a lot of trouble. The Moriartys, who lived not far from us, always used real rocks and stones and the crib would take up one whole corner of the kitchen.

The biggest crib of all, of course, was in the church in front of one of the side altars. Sister Margaret from the convent would be behind screens for weeks arranging and fixing it. Finally, during the first Mass on Christmas Day, the screens were taken aside for everyone to see. The children especially loved it and would visit it many times during Christmas. On the sixth of January, which we called Little Christmas or Women's Christmas, the figures of the Three Kings were put in and then the whole crib would be taken down a week or 10 days later. It was the sign that Christmas was really over.

St Francis and the Crib

St Francis of Assisi is said to have made the tradition of the Christmas crib popular. He wanted the people to really know the story of the birth of Jesus. In 1223 in the church of Creccio in Italy he built a life-size crib which included a real donkey and cow! The tradition of building a crib soon spread all over Italy and from there to many parts of the world. It is not so popular today, but it is the crib that tells us the reason we celebrate Christmas at all.

Christmas Crib

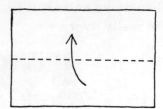

YOU WILL NEED

1 Sheet of 15 inch x 11 inch (38 x 28 cm) approx white cartridge paper
2 Some coloured paper. Coloured sugar-paper is ideal because it is firm

3 Paste

WHAT TO DO

A Fold cartridge paper as shown:

B Mark the centre point at the top and on either side. Draw in arch shape and cut.

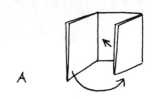

A

C Fold in two. Draw in shape and cut. Edges should be approx 1 1/2cm wide.

D Open out completely and cut sidepieces as shown.

E Cut out Mary, Joseph and Jesus from the sugar-paper. Paste to one of the centre arches, right side downwards.

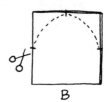

B

F Fold some green sugar-paper in four and cut four trees to fit arches. Paste them to the side arches, right side downwards.

G Fold crib over and paste the two centre arches together.

H Stand crib so that the front side arches open outwards and the back side arches inwards. See bird's eye view of crib.

I Slightly overlap back side arches and keep together with a dab of paste. In getting the crib to stand steadily, you may have to crease the side arches over and back where they meet the centre arch.

J Cut star from coloured or silver paper and paste to top of centre arch.

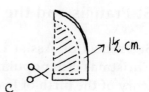

C

Joseph and the Gentle Mary

Joseph and the Gentle Mary
Went to David's royal city,
There there was no lodging for them,
For the poor there was no pity. Alleluia.

Through the streets they wandered weary,
Till at last they found a stable;
Joseph entered there with Mary,
And in that place was born our Saviour. Alleluia.

D , E , F

BACK SIDE-ARCHES

FRONT SIDE-ARCHES

BIRD'S-EYE VIEW OF CRIB

H

The Friendly Beasts

Jesus our brother, strong and good,
Was humbly born in a stable rude,
And the friendly beasts around him stood,
Jesus our brother, strong and good.

'I,' said the donkey, shaggy and brown,
'I carried his mother up and down,'
'I carried her safely to Bethlehem town;'
'I,' said the donkey shaggy and brown.

'I,' said the cow all white and red,
'I gave Him my manger for His bed,'
'I gave Him my hay to pillow His head:'
'I,' said the cow all white and red.

'I,' said the sheep with curly horn,
'I gave Him my wool for his blanket warm,'
'He wore my coat on Christmas morn;'
'I,' said the sheep with curly horn.

'I,' said the dove, from the rafters high,
'Cooed Him to sleep, my mate and I,'
'We cooed Him to sleep, my mate and I;'
'I,' said the dove from the rafters high.

And every beast, by some good spell,
In the stable dark was glad to tell,
Of the gift he gave Immanuel,
The gift he gave Immanuel.

12th Century carol

Away in a Manger

Away in a manger, no crib for a bed,
The little Lord Jesus laid down his sweet head:
The stars in the bright sky looked down where he lay,
The little Lord Jesus asleep on the hay.

The cattle are lowing, the baby awakes,
But little Lord Jesus, no crying he makes.
I love thee, Lord Jesus! Look down from the sky,
And stay by my side until morning is nigh.

Be near me, Lord Jesus; I ask thee to stay
Close by me for ever, and love me, I pray.
Bless all the dear children in thy tender care,
And fit us for heaven, to live with thee there.

A Cabin Cradle Song

Hush, *mo chroí*, hush,
The birds are asleep in the brush;
The stars are crowding the sky wi' their light
As they did long ago on Nativity Night.
Hush, *mo chroí*, hush.

Sleep, *mo chroí*, sleep.
Each hill holds its full o' white sheep.
Three Kings on their camels wi' treasure I see,
But love is the birth-gift my heart brings to ye.
Sleep, *mo chroí*, sleep.

Rest, *mo chroí*, rest.
Each mother that beareth is blest.
Hark, Mother Mary, look down as I pray,
And bless ye all childher at this ring o' day.
Rest, *mo chroí*, rest.

Ruth Sawyer

The Christmas Tree

There were no Christmas trees in the countryside when I was growing up though in the towns there would have been some. The first Christmas tree I ever saw was put up by a pair of returned Yanks - Mike and Noreen Gallagher. A returned Yank was the name we called somebody who had spent their life working in America, and then returned home to live in Ireland. They brought with them the customs they had got used to in America. The custom of decorating a tree at Christmastime comes from Germany, where they have been doing it for centuries.

The story goes that St Boniface had been trying to get the people in Germany to follow the message of Jesus. One winter he cut down a great oak tree they had been using as a place for pagan sacrifices. When he did, a little green fir tree began to grow in its place. He took this as a sign of hope for the future. Much later the custom spread to other countries.

It is not known whether this story is true or not, but ever since I saw that first Christmas tree I thought it was a very good idea. Christmas is at the very dead of winter, when the land lies resting and the days are at their darkest. The sun, if it shines at all, has only the strength and heat of a mirror flashing in the sky. The storms of January and February are ahead. Spring seems very far away. The tree, decorated and full of life, brightens the darkness of winter. It promises us that spring, with its new life, will come. The Christmas candle is for peace, the Christmas tree for hope.

Your Aunt Joan brought me most of these decorations from her travels around the world. I gave them to your Mum and Dad so that you young people could enjoy them. They make a really international Christmas tree. All the nations together celebrating the birth of Jesus.

Holland

These little gold and silver bells come from Holland. They ring out the good news that Jesus has been born. In Holland the children get most of their presents on the sixth of December, St Nicholas's Day, and not on Christmas Day. They leave their shoes or wooden clogs beside the fire or on the window sill and next morning they are filled with sweets and little presents.

Dutch Bells

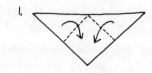
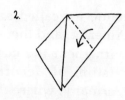

YOU WILL NEED

1 Fluorescent paper with a white backing

2 Thread for hanging

WHAT TO DO

A Cut the paper into 8cm squares.

B Crease diagonally, open, and cut into two triangles. Each triangle will give one bell.

C Fold as follows:

D Make a little hole at the top of each bell. Threading from the back, tie a double knot at the top of each one. Leave about 8cm between each bell.

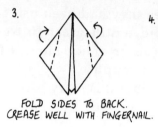

FOLD SIDES TO BACK.
CREASE WELL WITH FINGERNAIL.

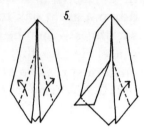

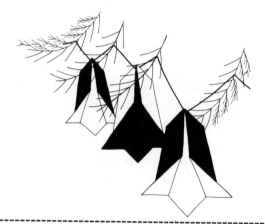

Switzerland

The brightly decorated star flowers come from Switzerland. In Switzerland the children get their presents from the 'Christkind', who is an angel that comes on Christmas Eve. On the Sunday before Christmas many towns have parades of carol singers, and people dress up as Mary and Joseph, shepherds, angels and the Three Wise Kings. On Christmas Eve, in the little villages in the mountains, they ring bells to welcome in Christmas. They can be heard in all the valleys.

Star-flowers

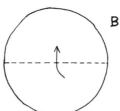
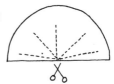

CUT, LEAVING A BORDER OF ABOUT 1½ CM.

YOU WILL NEED

1 Fluorescent or brightly-coloured paper with a white backing

2 Circular yoghurt carton, cup or compass for drawing circles. Circles should be about 7cm across

3 Coloured pencils or markers

OPEN FLAT AND FOLD POINTS BACK

WHAT TO DO

A Cut paper into circles.

B Fold each circle in two and cut as shown.

C Fold points back and crease with your nail. Decorate in a matching or contrasting colour.

D If you like, paste two together, back to back.

E Slip on to branch through centre hole, or hang with thread.

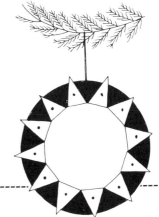

Finland

   The woven baskets and birds of peace come from Finland. We'll fill the baskets with sweets and everyone can have one on Christmas Day. Christmas is called 'Joulu' in Finland, and Christmas Eve is more important than Christmas Day. Santa visits each home on Christmas Eve before the children go to bed. While they are waiting for him they dress up as Santa's helpers in long red hats. When he arrives he asks the question, 'Are there any good children here?' The answer of course is always Yes! Then the presents are given out to everybody and before Santa leaves Christmas carols are sung.

Heart Baskets

YOU WILL NEED
1 White and coloured paper
2 Sellotape

WHAT TO DO

A Cut two shapes, one from the white paper and one from the coloured paper, using the template below.

B Fold shapes together and cut. The cut must be longer than the width of the shapes.

C Weave as shown.

D Cut a long strip for the handle from the coloured paper. Sellotape ends to the inside of the basket.

E Fill with sweets or a little present.

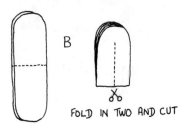

FOLD IN TWO AND CUT

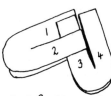

SLIP 3 THROUGH 2
AND 1 THROUGH 3

SLIP 2 THROUGH 4
AND 4 THROUGH 1

TEMPLATE FOR HEART-BASKETS

Bird of Peace

YOU WILL NEED

1 White paper and coloured paper. The body can be made from the coloured paper and the wings from the white, or vice versa. If possible, use a slightly heavier paper for the body

2 Hole puncher and thread for hanging

WHAT TO DO

A Cut out body shape using the template below.

B Punch a hole for the eye after first marking the place with a pencil.

C Cut a piece of paper about 9cm wide and 20cm long for the wings. Pleat, making pleats about 2cm wide. Fold in two and crease.

D Make a slit in the bird's body and slip pleats through. Do this carefully. Bring top ends of pleats together, above the bird's back. Make a hole through both top ends and tie them together with a length of thread. Use a double knot. Bring other ends down to fully open up pleats.

TEMPLATE FOR BIRD OF PEACE

Sweden

My favourite tree decorations are these Swedish crackers. I love the frilly ends. Christmas starts in Sweden on the thirteenth of December, St Lucia's Day, and ends on the fourteenth of January, St Knut's Day. On St Lucia's Day, which in Sweden was thought to be the longest night of the year, girls dress up in long white dresses with red sashes and wear a crown of lighted candles on their heads. Early that day they serve coffee and freshly baked buns to the family. Smaller children dress up as 'star boys', in pointed hats, and carry magic wands topped with stars.

Swedish Crackers

Once you have learned to make these crackers, they can be made in any size

YOU WILL NEED

1 Tissue or crêpe-paper in two contrasting colours **2** Piece of light cardboard

3 Length of wool in a matching colour to one of the papers

4 Silver stick-on stars, sellotape

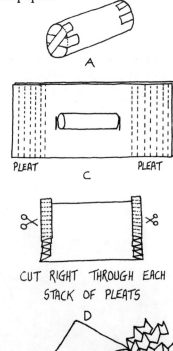

WHAT TO DO

A Cut a rectangle, 10cm x 12cm, from the cardboard. Roll into a tube and keep together with sellotape. Slip some sweets or a little present inside and put a piece of sellotape across each end to stop them falling out.

B Cut two pieces of tissue, one in each colour, 50cm long and 18cm wide. Put one on top of the other and put a tiny dab of paste in between to keep them together.

C Put the tube in the centre of the two sheets of tissue and mark its place lightly in pencil at either end. Pleat the sheets of tissue, in narrow pleats, to within 2cm of these marks.

D Cut pleats into narrow strips as shown.

E Fold the tissue around the tube and keep in place with paste.

F Tie one end of the piece of wool at one end of the tube, crushing the tissue together. Use a double knot. Then tie the other end of the wool at the other end of the tube. Shake tube to release pleats. Decorate with silver stars and hang.

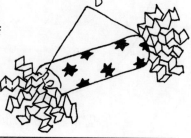

CUT RIGHT THROUGH EACH STACK OF PLEATS

Denmark

The cones and pretty see-through decorations come from Denmark. Like Finland, Christmas Eve is the important day for the Danes. Instead of plum pudding for dessert they have a rice pudding with an almond inside. Whoever gets the almond wins a special prize. After Christmas dinner the family hold hands and walk around the Christmas tree singing hymns and carols. Afterwards the presents from underneath the tree are given out.

In the Danish countryside people used to believe that little leprechauns called 'Nisse' helped to mind cows and horses. It's a tradition at Christmastime to leave a bowl of rice porridge for them in the barn. Otherwise the Nisse might begin to play tricks!

Christmas Cones

YOU WILL NEED

1 White paper or wrapping paper with a white backing. Paper should not be too light. Stripy paper makes a particularly nice cone

2 Length of wool in contrasting colour to your paper

3 Hole puncher, coloured pencils or markers

WHAT TO DO

A Cut paper into 10cm squares. If using white paper, decorate it using the coloured pencils or markers.

B Put paste down one edge, as shown, and fold into cone shape.

C Punch hole at top and thread with wool. Make a small bow from the wool and paste on. Fill with sweets, small presents or paper flowers.

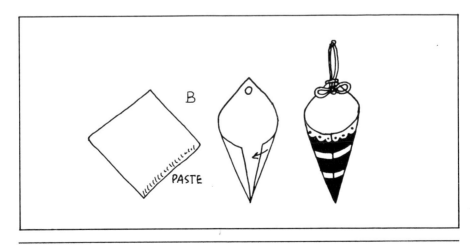

Christmas Windows

YOU WILL NEED

1 White paper and coloured paper

2 Coloured pencils or markers

3 Thread for hanging

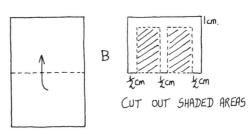

B

CUT OUT SHADED AREAS

WHAT TO DO

A Cut the white paper into rectangles of 5cm x 8cm.

B Fold in two and cut as shown. Open out flat.

C Cut out hearts, birds, stars, etc and paste to window, one on either side of the centre line.

D Decorate around the edge using the coloured pencils or markers. Put a hole at the top and hang.

E Instead of using white and coloured paper, two contrasting coloured papers can be used.

Spain

The little brightly coloured kites come from Spain. They remind me of warm sunshine. The most important day for Spanish children is the sixth of January. On that day they remember that the Three Kings brought presents to Jesus. The children put their shoes on the window sills or out on the balconies, hoping they will be filled with presents the following morning. And of course they always are! Just as you leave out a carrot for Santa's reindeer, they leave some straw for the Three Kings' camels.

Spanish Kite

YOU WILL NEED

1 Two drinking straws

2 Wool in two contrasting bright colours. Double-knitting wool is ideal

WHAT TO DO

A Cut two 10cm-long pieces from the straws.

B Cross the two pieces, and wind the wool around a few times to keep them together. Be sure you have a regular cross-shape.

C Continue winding as shown. Do not wind too tightly or the straws will bend. After a little while tie on the second colour and continue in that.

D Finish off by cutting a slit in the top straw-end and pulling the wool through. Tie a loop.

E Cut a few lengths of wool in each colour and tie them to the other ends. Hang.

F If making a larger kite, several colours can be used

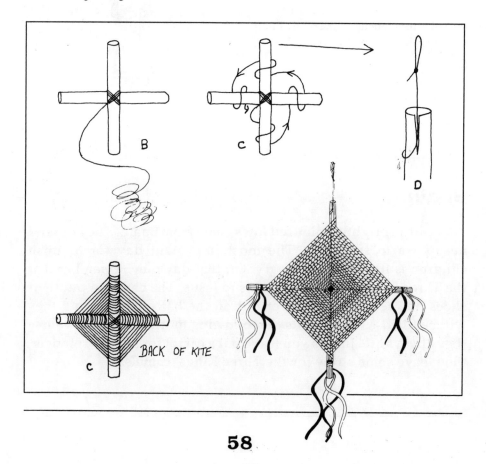

Germany

I've made these gingerbread biscuit ornaments just like they do in Germany. We'll wrap some of them in tinfoil so that they'll be fresh for eating on Christmas Day. In Germany the children get their presents not from Santa Claus but from an angel they call the 'Christkindl'. Bold children are supposed to be left a bundle of sticks - but of course there are never any bold children on Christmas night, are there?

Gingerbread Rings

These biscuits are easy to make and delicious to eat, but you will need an adult to advise you, especially about turning on the cooker and deciding when the gingerbread is cooked

YOU WILL NEED

8oz plain flour

4 1/2 oz margarine

4 oz soft brown sugar

2 oz black treacle

2oz golden syrup

1 heaped teaspoon of ground ginger

FOR THE DECORATION

2 full dessertspoons of cold water

9-10 heaped dessertspoons of instant royal icing

Smarties and little silver balls

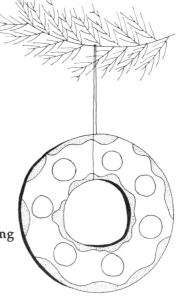

WHAT TO DO

A Wash your hands and be sure that all the utensils you use are clean.

B Put the oven on at 375°F/190°C/Gas mark 4. This is a fairly moderate oven.

C Cut the margarine into little pieces and put in a small saucepan over very low heat until it melts. This makes it easier to mix in later. Do not allow to boil or burn.

D Put all the ingredients in a large bowl and mix together well. Then knead the gingerbread with the palm of your hand until it is smooth and evenly coloured. Do this in the bowl.

E Shake some flour on the work-top and on your rolling pin. Roll out the gingerbread until it is about 1/2cm (5mm) thick.

F Cut into circles using a cutter, wine glass or cup. Each circle should be about 6 1/2cm across. Then cut a smaller circle from the centre of each large circle using a small cutter, screw-on bottle top, etc. The inner circle should be about 3cm across.

G Put biscuits on a baking tray. You can use a fish-slice to do this. Leave a space between each one as they spread slightly in cooking. Bake in oven for about 10-12mins. Check them after 10mins, making sure the underneath is not burned.

G Put biscuits on a cake rack to cool. When cold they can be iced.

TO ICE

A Put the water in a bowl and sprinkle the instant icing sugar over it.

B Beat with an electric hand-beater for about 7mins. The icing must be thick and creamy but able to flow. If it is too watery it will flow off the biscuits. Add more instant icing sugar to your mixture if this is the case.

C Decorate the biscuits in batches of three or four.

D Using a teaspoon, put a few generous dabs of icing around the top of each biscuit, smoothing it all around with the back of the spoon.

E Stick about five smarties on the icing, putting little silver balls in between.

F Leave to dry. Allow any excess icing to drip through the cake rack. It can be cleaned up later.

G When icing has set, tie each ring with thread and hang on the tree. If you are hanging them several days before Christmas, cover each one with tinfoil to keep them fresh. If you like, you can ice the other side of each biscuit as well, when the first side is dry.

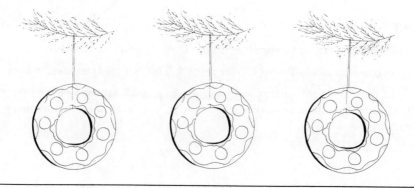

Stars

Last but not least we must put on the stars. The star for the top of the tree is an origami star from Japan, and the rest are from Germany, Sweden and Ireland. I learned to make the Irish one many years ago in Wexford.

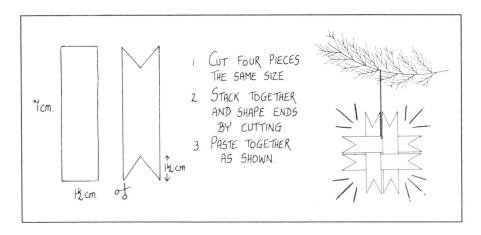

Swedish and German Stars

YOU WILL NEED

1 White paper, not too light. Cartridge paper is ideal

2 Paste

These are traditionally made from straw or bast, but here we will make them from white paper.

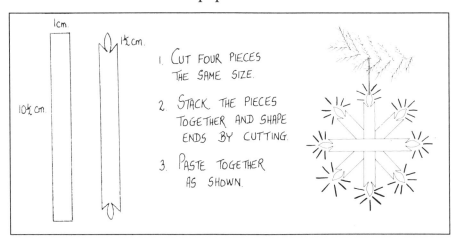

Irish Star
WHAT TO DO

1 Cut 4, 12 cm. lengths from the rushes.
2 Flatten each one with the edge of your nail.
3 Fold each one in two.

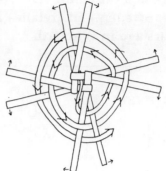

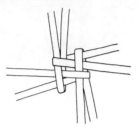

4 Weave the four lengths together as shown above. This is the same as starting a St. Bridget's cross.

5 Choose a long thin rush and weave it in and out as shown. Gently pull apart the folded rushes, as you weave, to form the star shape. When finishing, secure the end of the long thin rush by weaving it across the centre circle.

YOU WILL NEED

Use green rushes for these. Green rushes can be found growing in damp places, at the beach, near a river, in a bog. Ask your Mum or Dad to help you to find them. They are the same as those used in making St Bridget's crosses.

Japanese Star

This is an origami star from Japan and will look nice at the top of the tree. Christmas is not a traditional festival in Japan as it is here. Celebrating the beginning of the new year is more important to the Japanese.

YOU WILL NEED

Gold, silver or fluorescent paper with a white backing

WHAT TO DO.

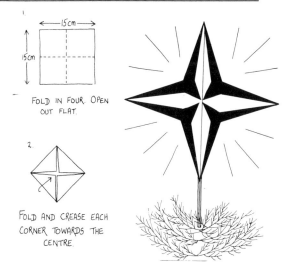

1. FOLD IN FOUR. OPEN OUT FLAT. (15cm x 15cm)

2. FOLD AND CREASE EACH CORNER TOWARDS THE CENTRE.

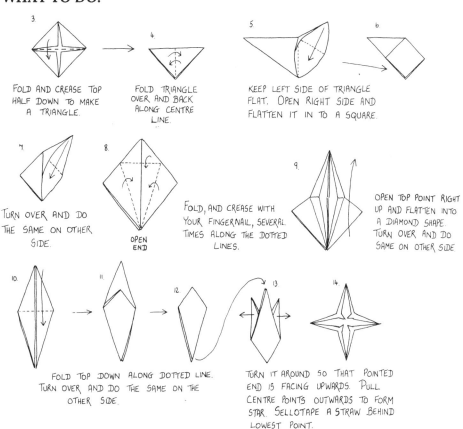

3. FOLD AND CREASE TOP HALF DOWN TO MAKE A TRIANGLE.

4. FOLD TRIANGLE OVER AND BACK ALONG CENTRE LINE.

5. KEEP LEFT SIDE OF TRIANGLE FLAT. OPEN RIGHT SIDE AND FLATTEN IT IN TO A SQUARE.

6.

7. TURN OVER AND DO THE SAME ON OTHER SIDE.

8. OPEN END. FOLD, AND CREASE WITH YOUR FINGERNAIL, SEVERAL TIMES ALONG THE DOTTED LINES.

9. OPEN TOP POINT RIGHT UP AND FLATTEN INTO A DIAMOND SHAPE. TURN OVER AND DO SAME ON OTHER SIDE.

10.

11. FOLD TOP DOWN ALONG DOTTED LINE. TURN OVER AND DO THE SAME ON THE OTHER SIDE.

12.

13. TURN IT AROUND SO THAT POINTED END IS FACING UPWARDS. PULL CENTRE POINTS OUTWARDS TO FORM STAR. SELLOTAPE A STRAW BEHIND LOWEST POINT.

14.

Turn on the lights and let Christmas begin!

The Carol Service

When I was a girl I had a great friend called Ruth Stafford - Auntie Ruth your Dad used to call her. She lived in the parsonage with her parents and brother. Her father was called Reverend Stafford and he was the vicar of St James's church, just across the fields from us.

Before Christmas, Ruth's family always made a wreath of ivy and spruce and put four candles on it. One candle was lit on each of the three Sundays before Christmas, and finally on Christmas Day all four would be lit. The wreath sat in the middle of the large dining room table and we children loved to watch it, especially when all four candles were lighting. This wreath reminds me of the Advent Calendar you made at school. It helps us prepare for Christmas, and lights up our way towards the big event.

Also, Ruth always took part in a Nativity play. This was held in the church. The story of Christmas was acted out in mime, and carols were sung about all the events of Christmastime - about the shepherds coming to find Jesus, about the Wise Men who came from foreign places. Every child had a part to play, and the whole congregation came to watch and to join with the children in the singing.

But the biggest event of all in their church was the carol service on Christmas Eve. This service is called the Nine Lessons and Carols. I will tell you all about it, and maybe this year we can go to St Patrick's Cathedral here in Dublin and join in this service. This is a big event in Dublin. The large church - do you know it is the longest church in Ireland? - is filled with hundreds of people, all singing carols together. Imagine the sound! The whole church is filled with music.

Nine readings are chosen from the Bible, and then carols are sung between each reading. The nine readings together tell us the whole story of the coming of Christ - waiting for his arrival, and then his birth.

The first carol is usually 'Once in Royal David's City'. Here is the first verse:

> Once in Royal David's City
> Stood a lowly cattle shed,
> Where a mother laid her baby
> In a manger for his bed;
> Mary was that mother mild,
> Jesus Christ her little child.

The first lesson is from Genesis, the first book of the Bible. It tells us about the fall of man into sin and the need for the saviour to come. Then, from the Book of Isaiah we hear of the promise of the saviour, and later we are told of the announcement to Mary of the birth of a son, who would be Jesus the saviour.

Between each lesson carols like 'Ding Dong! Merrily on High', 'I Saw Three Ships' and 'The Holly and the Ivy' are sung.

The eighth lesson tells us about the Three Wise Men led by a star to Bethlehem, and the ninth lesson is from the Gospel of St John, and it tells us of the meaning and importance of all the Christmas events. Usually the service ends with the carol 'Hark! The Herald Angels Sing', which is very bright and cheerful.

Ruth loved this service because she knew every carol very well. She taught them to me and I will teach them to you so you can sing them when we go to St Patrick's.

Epiphany

For Ruth's family, Epiphany, the sixth of January, was also a very pleasant day. I was always invited to her house on that day for mince pies and lemonade.

Before we had the mince pies Ruth's father always reminded us that on this day we were remembering the Three Wise Men. They had gone home, far away from Bethlehem with the message of Christmas, and this is the day when we remember all missionaries.

He reminded us that we children should think of the poor and needy on this day, and try to be generous in the coming year. And then we all tucked into the mince pies!

The Nativity play is much loved by children, but has its worrying moments for those organising it. Here is how Edna Burrows, who has prepared many Nativity plays, experienced it.

The Nativity Play

Each year, at the beginning of November, our thoughts turned, rather reluctantly, to the children's Nativity play which took place in the church on the Sunday after Christmas. We used to rack our brains for a new idea to dress up the traditional theme, for we knew that, whatever we did we must end up with the crib, Mary, Joseph, the shepherds, the Wise Men and the angels. That was the proper climax in the minds of small children, and no other would do.

If the plot was straightforward this was easy. For example the story of a donkey was no problem. After several adventures in his life he could turn out to be THE donkey that carried Mary. Or you

could do the Wise Men travelling from afar, one from the hills of
the north (the church gallery), and others from countries
represented by the west end and side aisles of the church.

However, if we launched into something more daring, such as using the musical *Oliver*, it took a bit of work to get to the proper end - the Nativity. But children are delightful in their readiness to accept an idea and their ability to enlarge on it. They saw nothing strange in running up and down the aisle asking grown-ups to 'consider themselves at home, consider themselves part of the family'. And indeed, what better feelings could be expressed about God's house? Nor did children find it odd that Mr Bumble, that man so horrid to the children in Oliver Twist's orphanage, should have a sudden change of heart because of a dream about the Nativity, so that he turned up with the shepherds, Wise Men, angels and all the children and knelt at the crib too!

Small girls love dressing up as angels. One prayed so hard every night that she would be chosen as one that her worried mother was greatly relieved when she was. Another, realising that angels didn't wear glasses, removed her spectacles! A real angel must have been watching over her as she moved in a long gown over a set of steps made of rather rickety boxes and hassocks. We learned afterwards that she had almost no vision at all without her specs.

Once they get past eight years of age boys usually prefer to help with the props, so it is hard to find one young enough to be willing to play Joseph and tall enough to pair with Mary. Older boys *can* be persuaded to be the back and front legs of the donkey! With Mary mounted, progress can be dangerous and, indeed, hilarious over the polished tiles of the chancel, and we never completed the journey at rehearsals without some mishap. I looked forward to 'the night' with some fear. But it is extraordinary how small children will rise to the occasion and they never failed to surprise me when I expected the worst. Their better selves emerge and, in this case, they carried their precious burden in triumph, the whole group looking strangely touching, helped by the sound of a real donkey's bray recorded on a cassette.

The bigger boys love rigging up props - one year the star travelled right across the church by means of a pulley stretched from one gallery to another! Then there was the occasion when the huge church ladder was mounted on a trestle table in the chancel to depict the ladder that Jacob saw in his dream. As I watched the small angels going up and down the ladder I was thankful that they were so light and that they were the children of parents who were as deep into amateur theatricals as I was myself.

Rehearsals were wearing. The church was always bitterly cold, and patient parents sat waiting while some parts of the performance were done over and over again. I used to wonder each year why I got involved, especially when I found myself on Christmas Day hemming a shepherd's cloak or making Herod's crown. We wondered if the whole thing would ever gel, if the children would remember to speak up, if Mary would remember not to leave the baby behind in the manger for the end procession. But if the unexpected mistake did happen - and it usually did - it was outweighed by the great reverence that little children have. This took over, and they moved gracefully and gently. They believed in what they were doing and even the two bold shepherds, who during rehearsals couldn't resist tweaking each other's headgear, wanted to do it well.

And when the small figures - shepherds, angels, Wise Men, and the group of very tiny shy ones who crept up the aisle at the last moment - knelt in adoration at the manger, something happened. Something to do with glory and innocence, something which, for those of us who had experienced the slog, was reward enough.

Edna Burrows

Santa Claus

San Nioclás - Daidí na Nollag

Of course the person you're all looking forward to is Santa Claus. He's the one that brings the presents and surprises. When I was growing up Santa Claus didn't visit us at all, but when your Dad was little he came every year. And oh! did your Dad look forward to him. Early to bed on Christmas Eve, leaving his stocking at the end of the bed. Up at the crack of dawn, playing with his new toys and waking up the whole household.

I remember one year he got a bus with people painted on the sides of it. All Christmas Day he worried about those people. Would they ever be able to get out? How would they get food? How would they get air? For ages he was upstairs, very quiet. Then we heard the howls. Down he came with the bus in pieces. He had tried to prise the people out of the bus with a screwdriver, but of course all he succeeded in doing was breaking it. He cried and cried and cried. Not even sweets would comfort him.

Santa's Many Names

We say in Ireland that Santa Claus comes on Christmas Eve in a sleigh pulled by reindeers. In Holland he arrives on the sixth of December in a steamship from Spain. They call him Sinterklaas. He comes with a helper called Black Peter. As soon as he arrives he gets on a white horse and visits every house. He asks the parents if the children have been good. Black Peter writes down the answers in a book. That night the good children are left presents and the bold ones get a bunch of sticks! Really bold children are put in a sack and taken back to Spain to help Santa prepare next year's presents. Or so it is said!

In Austria Santa Claus is known as Nikolo and has a helper called Krampus. In Finland he is called Joulupukki, in Norway,

La Befana, a white witch, visits Italian children

Julenissen, and in France, Père Noel.

However, it is not Santa Claus who brings the presents to Italian children but a white witch called *La Befana*. She is supposed to be one of the people who refused to give shelter to Mary and Joseph. Ever since, she has tried to make up for her bad deed by giving presents on the sixth of January every year.

Have you written your letter to Santa? Most children do so well before Christmas to give Santa time to prepare his gifts. But it can happen that you don't get what you want. Here's what Frank O'Connor did about that situation when he was a naughty little boy!

The Unwanted Gift

Coming on to dawn I woke with the feeling that something dreadful had happened. The whole house was quiet, and the little bedroom that looked out on the foot and a half of back yard was pitch-dark. It was only when I glanced at the window that I saw how all the silver had drained out of the sky. I jumped out of bed to feel my stocking, well knowing that the worst had happened. Santa had come while I was asleep, and had gone away with an entirely false impression of me, because all he had left me was some sort of book, folded up, a pen and a pencil, and a tuppenny bag of sweets. Not even Snakes-and-Ladders! For a while I was too stunned even to think. A fellow who was able to drive over rooftops and climb down chimneys without getting stuck. God, wouldn't you think he'd know better?

Then I began to wonder what that foxy boy, Sonny, had. I went to his side of the bed and felt his stocking. For all his spelling and sucking-up he hadn't done much better, because, apart from a bag of sweets like mine, all Santa had left him was a pop-gun, one that fired a cork on a piece of string and which you could get in any huxter's shop for sixpence.

All the same, the fact remained that it was a gun, and a gun was better than a book any day of the week. The Dohertys had a gang, and the gang fought the Strawberry Lane kids who tried to play football on our road. That gun would be very useful to me in many ways, while it would be lost on Sonny who wouldn't be let play with the gang, even if he wanted to.

Then I got the inspiration, as it seemed to me, direct from heaven. Suppose I took the gun and gave Sonny the book! Sonny would never be any good in the gang: he was fond of spelling, and a studious child like him could learn a lot of spellings from a book like mine. As he hadn't seen Santa any more than I had, what he hadn't seen wouldn't grieve him. I was doing no harm to anyone; in fact if Sonny only knew I was doing him a good turn which he might have cause to thank me for later. That was one thing I was always keen on; doing good turns. Perhaps this was Santa's intention the whole time and he had merely become confused between us. It was a mistake that might happen to anyone. So I put the book, the pencil and the pen into Sonny's stocking and the pop-gun into my own, and returned to bed and slept again.

The Stories of Frank O'Connor

Christmas Day

Christmas Morning

Christmas day was always special. The whole world seemed happy. Good cheer was in the very air we breathed.

We would wake up in the dark of the cold morning, excited, and go straight down to the kitchen to dress in front of the fire. Mother would already be up and working, wearing her new apron. She always bought herself a new apron for Christmas.

Then off we would go to early Mass. Most people walked to Mass in those days. You would hear them coming along in the dark before you saw them.

The grown-ups would wish one another 'Happy Christmas' and the answer was always 'Many happy returns'.

In some houses the Christmas candle would be lighting in the window and you could sneak a look inside at their decorations and the cards hanging up.

Reaching the church, the lights always seemed extra bright in the dark morning. We were in such a Christmas mood that we wouldn't have been surprised to hear angels singing. The altar was always specially decorated and the priest wore the golden vestments. We children half-slept through Mass only interested in the visit to the crib afterwards. Then it was off home to breakfast and the Christmas dinner to look forward to.

In earlier times the men and older boys from different parishes would play a hurling match against each other while the women stayed at home to prepare the dinner.

During the morning neighbours and relations coming home from a later Mass might call in, but by one or two o'clock every family stayed in their own house and celebrated Christmas with whatever food or drink they had.

Dashing through the snow

The Christmas Goose

Christmas is coming and the geese are getting fat,
Please put a penny in the old man's hat,
If you haven't got a penny a halfpenny will do,
If you haven't got a halfpenny, God bless you.

When I was a child we always managed a goose with potato stuffing for Christmas dinner. Not every household would have one. Some people would have had to make do with a bit of dried fish in white sauce or a piece of salty bacon.

Mother always called the goose 'the Bird', making it sound very important. Plucking the feathers from the dead goose was a very big event. It had to be done properly without tearing the bird's skin. There was a special knack to it just like milking a cow.

My older brother Peter was the best at doing it in our house. He would sit on a box, in one of the out-houses, the bird across his lap and feathers all around him on the ground and rising above him in the air. We younger ones would stand at the door watching him in admiration. With a firm gentle tug he would take off the feathers and you knew from the low tearing sound that they were coming away cleanly.

The feathers were carefully kept to stuff pillows and eiderdowns and the wings were used as little dustpan brushes. It was a far cry from today's frozen turkeys.

The Plum Pudding

Flour of Ireland, fruit of Spain
Met together in a shower of rain;
Put in a bag, tied up with string
If you tell me this riddle I'll give you a ring.

The plum pudding was made two months or so before Christmas. In fact Mother always made a few and we would have one on New Year's Day and Little Christmas (the sixth of January) as well.

We would arrive home from school to find her in the kitchen weighing and picking and washing and examining the fruit - mounds of currants, raisins, candied peel and almonds. All would be mixed together with a bottle of porter (Guinness) in two large mixing-bowls, one of them on loan from one of the neighbours. Everyone helped with the stirring and as you stirred you could make a wish. Then the mixture was put into bowls and the top covered over with a cloth and tightly tied. Then the boiling of the puddings started, and to us children it seemed very long and very mysterious. There was always great fuss and discussion about whether they were cooked or not. Afterwards they were stored on the wide window-sill at the turn of the stairs. Sacred bundles of waiting delight. We children were sternly warned not to poke or pick at them. On Christmas Day, Pa would splash a little whiskey or *poitín* over the top of the pudding and set it alight as mother brought it across to the table.

Christmas in Belfast city in olden days was, of course, a time for visiting friends and relations. Here, Alice Kane tells about the family visit to Aunt Jennie's on Christmas Day when she was a child.

Christmas Dinner in Belfast

At Christmas we really feasted. Aunt Jennie had a big old house downtown and after we had opened our stockings and forced some breakfast down, we went to Aunt Jennie's for dinner. The tramcars were off for the holiday, so the Station Cab Company sent a vehicle, booked well in advance, to take us to Great Victoria Street. Sometimes it was a taxi; motorcars were rare and a treat to us; and sometimes it was a sidecar, known in song as a jaunting car. We never could decide which we liked best: the taxi, so shiny, so modern, but so terribly fast, or the more leisurely old-fashioned sidecar, clip-clopping through the empty street . . .

When we arrived at Aunt Jennie's it was festive indeed. Uncles and aunts and cousins from near and far had come from Belfast and Larne and Bangor, Dublin, and even England. Presents were exchanged and the children ran up and down stairs, opened parcels, played all manner of games, and sneaked sweeties before dinner, and occasionally stole downstairs to the kitchen to see how things were coming along. In Irish fashion the enormous turkey was always accompanied by a big ham, covered with mustard and buttered breadcrumbs, and stuck with cloves, as well as bacon and strings of plump little pork sausages. (Fowl alone was not considered much of a dinner.) Also, there was always bread sauce and riced potatoes and vegetables and then the wonderful rich satisfying dessert to complete the feast; plum pudding and mince pie and apples and nuts and muscatel raisins.

Songs and Sayings of an Ulster Childhood, by Alice Kane,
edited by Edith Fowke

Silent Night

Silent night, holy night,
All is calm, all is bright
'Round yon virgin mother and child
Holy infant so tender and mild
Sleep in heavenly peace, sleep in heavenly peace

'Silent Night' must be the most famous of all Christmas carols. It was written in 1818 in the little Austrian village of Oberndorf. The church organ had been broken on Christmas Eve and the parish priest, Father Joseph Mohr, was very worried that there wouldn't be any music for the midnight Mass. He quickly sat down and there and then wrote the words of a new hymn. He asked his friend, Franz Gruber the schoolmaster, to write the music, to be sung by the choir and accompanied on guitar. 'Silent Night' was ready by the time Mass began, and has since become a firm favourite all over the world. It was originally written in German as 'Stille Nacht'.

'The Wexford Carol' is sung at Christmas in different parts of County Wexford. It is one of the few traditional Irish carols and tells the story of Christmas from the birth of Jesus until the coming of the Three Kings. It is sometimes known as the 'Enniscorthy Christmas Carol'.

The Wexford Carol

Good people all, this Christmas time,
Consider well and bear in mind,
What our good God for us has done,
In sending His beloved Son.
With Mary holy we should pray
To God with love this Christmas Day;
In Bethlehem upon that morn
There was a blessed Messiah born.

The night before the happy tide,
The noble Virgin and her guide
Were a long time seeking up and down
To find a lodging in the town.
But mark how all things came to pass,
From every door repelled, alas!
As long foretold, their refuge all,
Was but an humble ox's stall.

Near Bethlehem did shepherds keep
Their flocks of lambs and feeding sheep
To whom God's angels did appear,
Which put the shepherds in great fear.
'Prepare and go' the angels said,
'To Bethlehem, be not afraid
For there you'll find this happy morn,
A princely Babe, sweet Jesus born.'

With thankful heart and joyful mind,
The shepherds went the Babe to find.
And as God's angels had foretold,
They did Our Saviour, Christ, behold.
Within a manger He was laid,
And by His side the Virgin Maid,
Attending on the Lord of Life
Who came on earth to end all strife.

There were three wise men from afar,
Directed by a glorious star,
Came boldly on and made no stay
Until they came where Jesus lay.
And when they came unto that place
And looked with love on Jesus' face,
In faith they humbly knelt to greet
With gifts of gold and incense sweet.

Traditional

In Holland Santa arrives on a white horse

Why is Christmas Day on the 25th of December?

The exact time of year that Jesus was born is not really known. Early Christians disagreed so much on when to celebrate it that eventually in the fourth century Pope Julius I decided that the birth of Jesus would be remembered on the same day each year - the 25th of December.

He had good reasons for choosing this date. Long before Jesus was born people in many countries had celebrations around the 21st of December, the shortest day in the year. This is called the winter solstice. On that day we get the least amount of sunlight, but from then onwards we have longer hours of light each day and soon afterwards spring begins to appear. Different peoples celebrated the coming of this new light and life in different ways.

The Romans had the festival of Saturnalia in honour of the gods of seeds and sowing. During the festival nobody was allowed to work except cooks and bakers! People decorated their houses with holly, ivy and lighted candles, and gave each other presents. They dressed up in fancy dress and had seven days of fun.

The Vikings had the festival of Yuletide in honour of Odin, the father of their gods. They decorated their houses with corn and straw, and made sacrifices to Odin so that they might have a good harvest in the coming year.

In northern Europe, where the days get really dark, huge bonfires were lit to drive away evil spirits and to welcome the new sun and the new life.

As all these festivals celebrated the coming of new life it seemed a good time to celebrate the coming of Jesus.

Many of the old customs were given Christian meanings. Candles came to mean Jesus, the Light of the World. Holly was a reminder of the crown of thorns. Straw remembered that Jesus was born in a stable. Giving presents remembered that Jesus was

God's gift to mankind.

These Christmastime celebrations continued down the centuries. Other customs developed and were added to the festival. Christmas came to be celebrated for twelve days. On Christmas Eve the biggest log that would fit in the fire was carried into the house and lighted from a piece of the previous year's log. It was known as the Yule log and was another reminder of light and new life. Horses were blessed on the day after Christmas, St Stephen's Day. Groups of actors and singers called mummers went around from village to village acting out plays. Everyone ate and drank as much as they could during the twelve days. On the Twelfth Night, the end of the Christmas festival was marked with a great banquet.

During the seventeenth century when the Puritans ruled in England, all festivals including Christmas were banned. Many of the old customs died then and it wasn't until the last century that some were revived again and new ones added. Christmas trees and plum puddings, presents and crackers, Santa Claus and reindeers, Christmas cards and decorations all became popular.

They are still with us today and seem very much here to stay.

The Wran's (Wren's) Day

The day we really looked forward to was not Christmas Day but the day afterwards - St Stephen's Day, or the Wran's (Wren's) Day as we called it. That was the day we all dressed up in whatever old clothes and hats we could find, wore a mask or a piece of an old lace curtain to cover our faces, and went around from house to house singing, dancing, playing music and collecting money. The group of people were called the 'wran', and the people in it called wranboys. When we stopped at a house we'd chant a little verse:

> The wran, the wran, the king of all birds,
> St Stephen's Day he was caught in the furze,
> So out with the fiddle and up with the drum,
> And give us a penny to bury the wran.

Most households would give you a few shillings to put in the box and by the end of the day there'd be quite an amount of money to share out.

For weeks beforehand everyone would be secretly getting together their costume, or rig-out as we used to call it. We'd ask each other - 'Have you a rig for the wran?' And of course everybody would say, 'No!' and keep it secret until the day. Only your best friend would know what you were going to wear.

When your father was growing up he always went out in the wran. We were living in the town then and it was a very exciting place on St Stephen's Day. There was an air of freedom and wildness about.

Every street had its own wran. About eleven o'clock in the morning each group of wranboys would gather together at their own meeting place. When they were ready they would march around the town to show themselves off. First would come two wranboys holding a banner showing the name of the wran - the Green and Gold, The Goat Street Wran, the John Street Wran, The

The wrenboys in high spirits

Quay Wran - every wran had its own name. Then came the wranboys dressed in their costumes and kept in order by the captain who would be running up and down with a long stick or wooden sword in his hand. The people watching the wrans would enjoy themselves trying to guess who was in each costume.

After that came the *Láir Bhán* or Hobby Horse. When it appeared the little children would run screaming, half in terror and half in delight behind their parents, as the horse's wooden mouth snapped fiercely at them. They thought it would take a bite out of them or gobble them up.

Finally would come the strawboys dressed in skirts and hats made from straw, and the musicians. There would be a drummer and some fifes, and maybe tin-whistles and a melodeon.

After the first parade, each wran would do the round of the town several times during the day - dancing all the time, knocking at doors and collecting money.

In the evening, when everybody was tired, all the wrans would join together for one big parade around the town.

Then each wran counted its money and of course everybody was curious to know which wran had collected the most. The money might be divided out between the people who had been with the wran all day or else some weeks later there'd be a 'Ball Night' of singing and dancing and drinking and eating. It put a great finish to Christmas.

The *Láir Bhán* or Hobby Horse

The hobby horse is made from a wooden frame covered with white material. At the front is the horse's head and tacked to the end a long rope tail. A hole is cut in the horse's back and the person who carries the hobby horse puts his head through this and rests the frame on his shoulders. The horse's lower jaw can be snapped open and closed by pulling a wire on the inside of the frame. This opening and closing strikes terror in all the children.

The custom of the hobby horse is found not only in Ireland but also in Wales and the Isle of Man. Dressing up in this way for celebrations is a very old tradition in many parts of Europe.

Strawboys

The strawboys' costumes are made well in advance of St Stephen's Day. They consist of a skirt, top and head-dress. Bunches of golden straw are knotted onto lengths of twine and these lengths are then tied in a circle to make a waistband or neckband. The top of the headdress is tied tightly and finished off by plaiting the straw into two or three goat-like horns. The wearing of straw costumes for celebrations is a tradition not only in Ireland but in Britain, Spain and Portugal as well.

The Wrenboys also visited the 'Big House'. Here is a description from Coole Park, in the Sligo area.

The Wrenboys at Coole

Although the Wrenboys wore skirts, there was never a girl among them, but their heavy nailed boots never looked strange to us, because all the girls we saw wore the self-same boots on Sundays.

Granma kept a heap of small apples for the Wrenboys. When each troop of Wrenboys had performed its turn of songs and dance, which varied slightly, but which had to finish with:

> The wran, the wran, the King of all Birds,
> St Stephen's Day was caught in the furze,
> Although he is small his family's great,
> Rise up kind lady and give us a treat.
>
> We followed him for a mile or more
> We followed him to Coole front door,
> Up with the kettle, down with the pan,
> Give us a penny to bury the wran.

she'd give the leaders a few coppers, and then with cries of 'Scib-scab, scib-scab' she'd throw handfuls of apples along the gravel. The Wrenboys madly rushed after them, fighting and scrambling to get as many as they could, heaving up their skirts to put what they couldn't carry into the pockets of their breeks underneath.

From Me and Nu, Anne Gregory

The Pantomime

In the cities after Christmas comes the outing children look forward to - the panto. This is a tradition that goes back many years. Paddy Crosbie remembers from the 1920s.

The Panto Long Ago

Christmas, however, was never Christmas without the Pantomime.

> Yez can keep your cowboy pictures,
> I can see them any day;
> I could do without me comic cuts
> Or a jaunt on Markey's dray.
> But there's one thing that I'd hate to miss
> If I did I'd feel, well, queer,
> It's when me father brins the family
> To the Pantomime each year.

The pantomimes were to be seen in all the theatres except the Theatre Royal. Our regular was the Olympia, but we were also brought to the Tivoli and the Queens. In our own area, a Christmas panto was presented annually in the Father Mathew Hall in Church Street, and I remember going on three occasions with a crowd of boys to the Boys' Brigade Hall in Lower Church Street, near the old church of St Michan's. The favourite panto was *Cinderella*.

Outside of the city theatres were to be found young hawkers

with leaflets, which they waved as they shouted 'Pantomime Songs a Penny, Pantomime Songs a Penny'. And every year without fail came the fellow with the peaked cap who sang 'One of the Old Reserves' to the queues. . . .

The barrel organ also made its appearance at the pantomime queues and there was another regular with a mouth-organ who never played any tune but the one 'Show Me the Way to Go Home'. But the waiting seemed an eternity.

At last the doors are opened
And me father pays for all,
He takes young Gaby in his arms,
An' up the steps we crawl.

It's an awful journey upwards,
Though us kids go in 'leps',
But me mudder pants an' me father laughs,
An' he says, 'Gerrup them steps'.

At last we reach the gallery;
We rush down to the front,
Last year our Mossy slipped an' fell,
An' got an awful dunt.

We sit down on our overcoats,
'Cause the seats are like cement,
An' then out loud we read and spell
Each big advertis'ment.

The conductor comes out smilin',
The lights go dim, then out,
The band strikes up a marchy tune,
An' someone starts to shout.

The curtain rises slowly,
We see a village green,
An' we all just sit there starin',
'Cause its like a lovely dream.

One year there was a 'divil',
An' he used to disappear;
A hole used open in the floor -
It made Hell seem awful near.

But the divil was fat and got stuck that night,
Though he tried to push and pull,
Then a voice from the gallery shouted out
'Three cheers, the place is full.'

Me mother an' me father,
They love the Pantomime,
An' when the funny man appears,
They laugh at every line,

An' me mudder loves the music too,
An' when a man appears,
Who sings songs like 'Nellie Dean',
Her eyes fill up with tears.

From Your Dinner's Poured Out, Paddy Crosbie

Maureen Potter is the best-known pantomime actor in Ireland. For forty years she has appeared at the panto in the Gaiety, rarely missing a year. In that theatre lived a cat. His name was Tommy, and his job was to keep the theatre free of rats and mice. Maureen has written the story of this Theatre Cat, told from the point of view of the cat. Here is a chapter:

The Man in the Cat

Tommy was dozing in his big red chair. The theatre was empty, but on the stage he could hear people talking and, in the background, the sound of hammering. That meant they were preparing for a show . . .

Suddenly he heard a voice calling, 'Tommy, Tommy, come along, please.'

I must be dreaming, he thought. Usually at this time the cry was, Get that cat out of here!

Then the voice again, 'Tommy, Tommy. Cat on stage, please.'

Tommy peeped over the edge of the box, and to his amazement the biggest cat he had ever seen bounded on to the stage. Tommy had never known his brothers and sisters, but often at night he looked out the windows and saw other cats passing silently across the waste ground opposite the theatre. They seemed to be the same size as himself, but this cat on stage was the biggest cat he had ever seen. And it was walking on its hind legs! He almost toppled out of the box in surprise.

The monster was being introduced to someone Tommy recognised - the small lady with glasses who often moved into the room beside the stage with the name 'Maureen Potter' on the door. A friendly lady who always had a pat for him and let him settle down on her couch as long as he did not lie on her clothes. Once, in a kittenish mood, he had played with some ribbons and knocked down a head of hair, and the small lady got very cross indeed. But she was usually a very friendly person.

And she must be a very brave one too, for there she was holding the paw of this huge cat. Then, music started up and the pair began to dance. Tommy looked on, eyes like saucers, feeling very small indeed. If this creature could do all these things, Tommy would soon be out of a job. What mouse or rat would venture in while a cat that size was at large? And to think it had taken his name too!

Everyone finally moved off stage, and Tommy ventured out of his hiding place to get a closer look at the intruder. He saw the big cat go into a dressing room, so he settled down on the landing above to watch. Shortly afterwards the door opened and Tommy crouched down nervously, but only a small man with glasses emerged. The man left the door open behind him, and after a while Tommy padded quietly downstairs and peeped into the room. There was no sign of the monster. Tommy crept cautiously inside. Then he almost died of shock, almost lost several of his nine lives. The monster was hiding behind the door! Tommy was trapped. He dashed under a table and prepared to defend himself. But no attack came, and eventually, nervously, he peeped out. The monster was still behind the door, but he looked flat and very still. Perhaps he was asleep? Perhaps Tommy could slide past him to safety?

Tommy was just at the door when he heard footsteps. It was the man returning. Tommy darted back under the table. Then, in a big mirror on the wall, he saw the man take off his shoes, put his glasses on the table, and then . . . and then . . . he climbed into the cat! The giant gazed at himself in the mirror, then left the room. Tommy was horrified. There was a man in that huge cat! Was there a man in every cat? Was there a small man inside *him* waiting to get out? He opened his mouth very wide and stared into the mirror. He could not see any man down there, only his red tongue and shining teeth. How did the man get past those sharp teeth when he wanted to get out?

Suddenly Tommy realised that there was someone looking at him from the doorway. It was the big cat, but this time it had a man's face - a smiling face.

'Hello, puss,' said the face, 'you must be Tommy. I'm delighted to meet you.' He put out a big paw and Tommy backed into a corner, snarling nervously.

'Does this frighten you? Here, I'll take it off.'

With that the man stepped out of the skin, for that is what it was. He laid it on the floor and said, with a laugh, 'C'mon, Tommy, have a good look at it.'

After much thought Tommy sniffed at the thing on the floor and then touched it with an uneasy paw. It was soft and furry, just like the white rug in front of the fire in that nice warm room upstairs. He had been in there once but a large man with a pipe had chased him away, shouting loudly to his old foe, the cleaning lady, 'Get that cat out of here.' Tommy walked across the skin, and, now much braver, began to shake and worry that big face and whiskers that had worried him so much before.

'Hold on, Tommy,' said the man, with a grin, 'that's my living you're attacking. Here, have a nice piece of chicken.'

He picked out a piece of chicken from his sandwich and put it on the floor. Tommy moved to take it and the man stroked his back.

'What a lovely coat you have,' he said. 'I wish I had it.'

Tommy backed away from the food. Was this a trick to get his skin? The man laughed.

'Eat your food. I'm not after your fur. We cats must stick together.'

Just then a voice below called, 'Tommy, Tommy,' and the man, picking up the cat skin said, 'C'mon, partner, let's give them a double act.' Tommy followed him cautiously downstairs and when they walked on stage together everyone laughed.

'I see you have an understudy, Terry,' said the small lady with the glasses, picking Tommy up and giving him a hug. So, the man in the cat was called Terry.

But a tall man in a sweater interrupted the fun.

'Right, Terry,' he said, 'Dick Whittington has put his bundle up in this tree. See if you can reach it.'

The cat man got down on all fours, stretched up a paw, but could not reach the bundle. I could reach that, thought Tommy, and with a quick spring he shot up the tree and knocked down the bundle. Unfortunately, the stage tree was not made for climbing and with a loud clatter the tree and Tommy both came crashing onto the stage. Everyone laughed again, except the stage hand who had to sort out the mess and the director who wanted to get on with the rehearsal. So Tommy was put in the wings to watch his new-found friend go through his paces. Every now and again Terry came over, patted him and asked, 'How am I doing, partner?'

Tommy and Terry became close friends and every night Tommy waited at the stage door for his cat man to arrive. He would follow him up to the dressing room and sit beside the mirror while Terry prepared for the show. Then he'd settle at the side of the stage and watch critically while Dick Whittington and his Cat went through all their adventures. Tommy purred with delight when Dick was made Lord Mayor of London and told all the audience that he could not have succeeded without his faithful Cat.

One night as Tommy waited at the stage door for his friend, he noticed sadly that lots of flowers were being delivered to the theatre. He knew from experience that this meant the show was coming to an end. For some reason he could never understand, the stage people gave one another flowers on the last night, and the following day they were all gone. So he watched with a heavy heart as Dick Whittington and his Cat went through the story he knew so well.

When the curtain was down and the show was finally over, Tommy went to visit his friend and found him packing away his cat suit in a basket. The room looked cold and lonely without the clothes and bottles and brushes that had become so familiar. Terry, reading Tommy's thoughts, said, 'I wonder who will be here next week?' Then he picked Tommy up, gave him a pat, and said, 'Come along, I have something to show you'.

He carried him across the stage, and there, in a quiet corner, was a little wooden house with the name TOMMY painted across it. The doorway was a flap that could be pushed open and on it was a star.

'It's your own dressing room,' said Terry. 'Go in and have a look.'

Tommy pushed open the flap and inside was a carpet made of the same material as the cat suit that had frightened him so much before. He sniffed all around the cosy interior and when he came out his friend had gone.

Tommy watches every year when the winter comes to see if the pantomime will have a cat in it. His friend has not returned since, but every Christmas a card arrives with the simple message, 'Happy Christmas, Tommy, see you again someday.' Fred, the stage doorman, pins the cards up on the wall of Tommy's 'dressing room'. The cards come from theatres all over the world, but Tommy is hoping that one Christmas it won't be a card that arrives but instead his old friend the Man in the Cat.

From The Theatre Cat, Maureen Potter

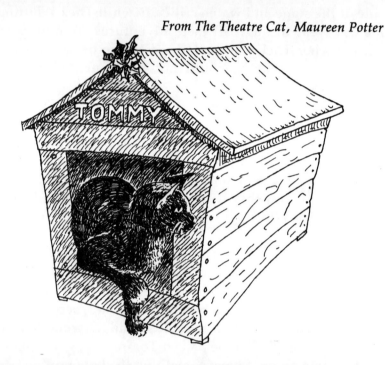

Acknowledgements : *Jimeen, An Irish Comic Classic*, Pádraig O Siochfhradha, translated by Pat Egan, Peter Fallon, Ide ní Laoghaire; *Your Dinner's Poured Out*, Paddy Crosbie; *Gur Cake and Coal Blocks*, Eamonn MacThomáis; *Old Days Old Ways*, Olive Sharkey; *The Theatre Cat*, Maureen Potter have all been published by The O'Brien Press. We thank the following for permission to reproduce other extracts: Wolfhound Press for *Songs and Sayings from an Ulster Childhood*, Alice Kane, edited by Edith Fowke; Victor Gollancz for 'The China Doll', from *The Far Side of the Lough*, Polly Devlin; The Bodley Head for 'A Cabin Cradle Song', Ruth Sawyer; A.D.Peters for *The Stories of Frank O'Connor*; Colin Smythe for *Me and Nu*, Anne Gregory. Every effort has been made to trace copyright holders. We would be happy to amend any oversight.